ROUTINES

Other books by Lawrence Ferlinghetti

Pictures of the Gone World (*Poems*)
A Coney Island of the Mind (*Poems*)
Her (*Novel*)
Paroles *by Jacques Prévert* (*Translation*)
Have You Sold Your Dozen Roses? (*Filmscript*)
Starting From San Francisco (*Poems*)
Unfair Arguments with Existence (*Plays*)

ROUTINES

Lawrence Ferlinghetti

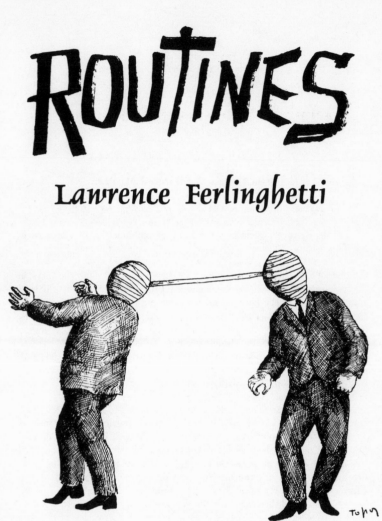

A New Directions Paperbook

ACKNOWLEDGMENTS: Some of these plays first appeared in *Red Clay*, *New Directions 18*, and *City Lights Journal 2*. Cover drawing and illustrations by Topor, courtesy of *El Corno Emplumado* (Mexico City) and Alacena, Editiones Era, publishers of *Cuentos Panicos* (Mexico City). The speech "What is a man?" in "Our Little Trip" is quoted from *Nine Chains to the Moon* by R. Buckminster Fuller (Copyright © 1963 by R. Buckminster Fuller); the author thanks Mr. Fuller and Southern Illinois University Press, publishers of *Nine Chains to the Moon*, for permission to use this passage.

Second Printing
Book Design by Gertrude Awe/Jean Krulis
Manufactured in the United States of America

New Directions Books are published for James Laughlin by New Directions Publishing Corporation, 333 Sixth Avenue, New York 14.

Contents

ROUTINES

Notes *on* ROUTINES . . . .

A "routine"—a song & dance, a little rout, a routing-out, a
run-around, a "round of business or amusement": myriads
of people, herds, flowerbeds, ships & cities, all going through
their routines, life itself a blackout routine, an experimental
madness somewhere between dotage and megalomania, lost
in the vibration of a wreckage (of some other cosmos we
fell out of). . . .

Routine happenings turned into dramatic action adding up
to Something. Hurry, hurry, hurry, the show's about to
begin to turn into Something Else. See the Bearded Lady
& your lives stretched out before you & added up for you
. . . Routine happenstances that *turn out to be* crises,
catharses, epiphanies, confrontations, manifestations, moments of truth, fatal instants (with the actuality of news-
paper clippings: THREE SAIL ATLANTIC IN OPEN BOAT),
pure inventions & pure creations of the pure creative imagination, true realities & true nightmares, panic gods & panic
clowns, destructions & disruptions, liberations (from all the
old hang-ups—phenomenological, neurotic, Reichian, liter-
ary, theatrical, political), liberating catastrophes, cut-ups
of existence, black masses & blackouts, flips, orgasms, erec-
tions & resurrections, pot dreams & visions . . . nexuses of

ordinary dramatics, nubs of normal plays, "obligatory scenes" complete in themselves, demonstrations & discoveries of those "secret relationships between things which seem to have no rapport at all" (Roger Blin on Genet), and "heightened fantastic projections of people, places, and actions" (Alan Ansen on William Burroughs). . . .

Routines on the bare boards of a kind of Third Stream Theatre (re the Third Stream Jazz scene): a "third stream" between oldstyle dramas & spontaneous Action or improvisation, between Well Made Plays (with their coherent pictures of coherent worlds which now turn out to be the falsest) and those free-form Happenings made of primitive perceptual chaos in which "nothing is coherent or formulated and the activity is without premeditation or afterthought, like some form of life prior to the development of the fore-brain, plankton or paleolithic" (from a description in *The Village Voice*) . . . A transition from the pure cathartic Happening or pseudo-event (often vapid, often psychopathic in essence; i.e., the classic cliché of chopping up a piano) and from Artaud's "theatre of latent barbarism" in which "one doesn't act, one takes action" and in which we are all cast as victims burnt at the stake "signalling through the flames" . . . Transition from all this so-necessary dramatic anarchism to pure Poetic Action not necessarily logical or rational but with, at best, that kind of inexpressible inchoate meaning that springs from wild surmises of the imagination. . . .

And all to make you "think of life." Not a theatre of pseudo-events (which daily newspapers already are) and not a "theatre for madmen only" yet a visionary theatre,

theatre as genesis of creation, working (or playing) toward revolutionary solutions, or evolutionary solutions, acting out aspirations to some ideal existence. And not always with words, speech itself but a paraphrase of thought, and even in pure miming an "inner speech" to be heard. . . .

With the strangest problem still how to get real depth of emotion into such visually exciting & seemingly superficial scenes . . . "For what," said Cabeza de Vaca, "can describe a happening in the shadows of the soul?"

Topor is Polish-French & lives in Paris but is one of the prime movers & shakers in "Los Panicos," a group in Mexico concerned with revolutionary art & theatre. His drawing on the cover of this book came out originally in *El Corno Emplumado* (Mexico City) from which arose the original idea of "Our Little Trip," just as another Topor drawing herein inspired the routine called "His Head" . . . The speech in answer to the question "What is a man?" near the beginning of "Our Little Trip" is taken from R. Buckminster Fuller's *Nine Chains to the Moon* (Southern Illinois University Press) . . . The conception of the furnace-statue in "Ha-Ha" came from a drawing by Heinrich Kley (Dover Books) . . . The final image of "Sleeper" is inscrutably related to Henri Rousseau's "La Bohémienne Endormie" & to his written description of that painting . . . The image of the Apple Seller in "The Center for Death" is taken from Albert Cossery's *Men God Forgot*. A certain group of people (whom I will not name for fear of damaging them by my rather flippant treatment of their idea) actually has plans for a Center for Death on a Caribbean

island where terminal cases will go to take visionary hallu-
cinogens, under medical supervision, at the time of death.
(Aldous Huxley took such in his dying days.) The Graduate Student's speeches in "Servants of the People" are
adapted from a speech by Robert Scheer at a Cuban crisis
rally in San Francisco. . . . Other thefts I have made from
exciting kindred works now being spontaneously created in
several countries (for instance, *Décollage* #4, ed. Volf
Vostell, Cologne, 1964) are mostly too far from their original contexts for me to be able to credit them. So that I can
only apologize to those I have cunningly plundered, and
laugh. At certain pregnant periods in history, as has often
been noted, strangely similar products of the questing imagination spring up simultaneously in widely separated (or
politically partitioned) parts of the world. And the free spirit
barely recognizes its own face over the obscene boundaries.

Ferlinghetti

San Francisco
July 1964

Our Little Trip

The general public, the audience, or all those who come to "bear witness" to this moment of life are given blankets as they arrive & asked to lie down under them. They do. Naturally they stir restlessly.

After some time, two figures grunt & roll over & rise up. They are two men dressed in conservative suits with black ties & shoes. The curious thing about the relationship of these two quite representative beings is that a single bandage is stretched between them & wrapped completely around each of their heads. Grunting, they start to turn away from each other, unwinding the bandage from their heads as they separate. After a few turns they stop indecisively, turning this way & that.

FIRST FIGURE (*as if reciting*): Getting and spending we lay waste our trousers, and our little trip is rounded with a slip—into eternity—

SECOND FIGURE: Oh, she had the look of longing to lay her lips on me—

The Second Figure turns away from the First Figure. The First Figure turns toward the Second Figure. The Second Figure stops turning away. The First Figure continues turning toward the Second Figure. When they are close together again, with their bandage completely wrapped about their heads again, they fall to the ground & lie still under the blankets.

Now two more figures rise up, each swathed from foot to head in one long bandage. The wrapping begins at the head of each figure & is wound downward, so that the feet must be unwrapped first, then the legs, then the body, then the head. The curious thing about the relationship of these two quite ordinary beings is that it is the same bandage that enwraps the two of them, the cloth continuing from the feet of one to the feet of the other.

The figures succeed in standing separately but when they attempt to separate further, they fall over. They manage to stand again, but strain away from each other in a kind of stumbling dance, rotating away from each other and thereby unwinding their joint bandage.

Enter the Question Man with a microphone. He has a little sign that says: "THE QUESTION MAN." He thrusts the mike at the head of first one figure and then the other, shouting "How did you choose your mate?" Muffled replies from the figures are not distinguishable, and the Question Man continues repeating his single question as the figures continue to turn and unwind away from each other. It is seen now that one is a man & the other a woman, dressed conventionally. A loudspeaker bawls the following speech, and there is cheering in the background as if the speech were being given at a convention, and the Question Man continues his single question, following the two figures with his mike as they further turn and unwind away from each other.

SPEECH: What is a mate? What is a man? I say, what is man? "Man is a self-balancing, 28-jointed adapter-based biped; an electro-chemical reduction plant, integral with segregated stowages of special energy extracts in storage batteries, for subsequent actuation of thousands of hydraulic and pneumatic pumps, with motors attached; 62,000 miles of capillaries; millions of warning signal, railroad and conveyor systems; crushers and cranes (of which the arms are magnificent 23-jointed affairs with self-surfacing and lubricating systems, and a universally distributed telephone system needing no service for 70 years if well managed); the whole, extraordinarily complex mechanism guided with exquisite precision from a turret in which are located telescopic and microscopic self-registering and recording range finders, a spectroscope, *et cetera*, the turret control being closely allied with an air conditioning intake-and-exhaust, and a main fuel intake.

"Within the few cubic inches housing the turret mechanisms, there is room, also, for two sound-wave and sound-direction-finder recording diaphragms, a filing and instant reference system, and an expertly devised analytical laboratory large enough not only to contain minute records of every last and continual event of up to 70 years' experience, or more, but to extend, by computation and abstract fabrication, this experience with relative accuracy into all corners of the observed universe. There is, also, a forecasting and tactical plotting department for the reduction of future possibilities and probabilities to generally successful specific choice. . . ."

As the speech reaches its conclusion, the two figures have reached the opposite edges of the visible area, only their heads still wrapped in the cloth. The length of the bandage is stretched between them, and the Question Man runs back & forth between them with his mike. As the speech ends, the two figures disappear, off left & right, and the bandage between them goes limp & falls to the ground.

WOMAN'S VOICE (*offstage*): Kiss, kiss! Lushed at last! O, love!

MAN'S VOICE (*offstage*): Grope, grope! Saboteurs of ourselves!

QUESTION MAN (*shouting after one of the figures, exasperated*): There's a two-to-one chance you don't know *who* your mate is!

WOMAN'S VOICE (*offstage*): I didn't choose him, he chose me! (*High laughter.*)

QUESTION MAN (*running to other side and shouting at other figure*): Now listen here! In a revolutionary society such as you suggest, in a really revolutionary situation, is that old problem of for instance T. S. Eliot's "dissociation of sensibility" to be taken seriously? Is the problem of the non-communication of any two individuals as in for instance Samuel Beckett to be considered of any real importance in a revolutionary situation in which food and—

MAN'S VOICE (*offstage, singing*):
Oh we are wounded, wound, unwound!
Oh the way we wear each other down
Oh the way we wind each other up,
And wound each other, wind each other down. . . .

QUESTION MAN (*running to other side and shouting at other figure*): In a revolutionary society such as you propose, does it really matter if two individual people in it cannot ever seem to really *really* communicate? What difference does it make if— You think it's still important, do you? In spite of all, you think what you two or any such two succeed in communicating to each other personally is of some real value to— You— You still think the question of identity—of your identity or his identity or her identity or anyone's own identity is still important? As if—as if "identity" were actually something that really existed—as if identities of any kind had actually been proved to exist, as in a certain book on metaphysics by P. F. Strawson in which Individuals `are "re-identifiable identities" and sounds are spaceless objects and—

The long bandage rises from the floor and becomes taut again, and the two figures reappear at each side, their heads still wrapped in the cloth. The difference is that they are now otherwise naked. They are obviously changed persons and now strain toward each other, and turn toward each other, keeping the bandage taut between them as they separately wind themselves up in it again and bring themselves together again.

QUESTION MAN (*holding the mike up to first one and then the other*): Do you really—really still think it makes one iota of difference in the end what you do with your little old identity or how many times you succeed in communicating between you or don't succeed, or how often or how radically you change your own little personal identities, et cetera, et cetera? In a revolution, does it really matter, does it make any difference in the living end if there is no real communication between any two individuals, male or female, mother and father, brother and sister, lover and lover, or who knows what you are under your—under your—uh—skin—

MAN'S FIGURE: We all travel under wraps, but still—and yet—

WOMAN'S FIGURE (*as if reciting*): A salt doll diving into the sea will not be protected by a waterproof coat—

The two figures have now rewound themselves completely in their long bandage and stand close to each other but not touching.

MAN'S FIGURE: I am sorry to say that no definite destination seems to have been pinned to our carcasses—

WOMAN'S FIGURE: Still—still we have come a long way in our search for ecstasy—

QUESTION MAN (*holding mike up between them*): Perhaps now—now at last you will be able to give our audience your final answer—this audience which has not yet decided—this audience which is still waiting for—which has not as yet made up its mind which way—Perhaps you will now give it your final considered opinion in this matter which concerns us all—after a lifetime of experience, so-called—at the very end of your whole—little trip—your whole "revolutionary" experience, so-called— Will or will not the individual endure, the free ego, the individual identity, will it

always somehow manage to reassert itself in spite of
all, no matter what it has to go through, no matter
what it is subjected to, in spite of all—

The two figures press against each other, fall to the
ground and lie together, seeming to caress each other with
a low moaning.

(Blackout)

His Head

Blindfolded Man in open space . . . very tall . . . turns around & around . . . Little Girl, no more than three feet tall, walks in very slowly, bearing Head of beautiful woman on a stick. She holds it up straight in front of her & marches around Man with it, passing under his outstretched arms. There is a headless wailing in the distance. Little Girl runs off toward it. The wailing stops.

Enter a Little Boy, no more than three feet tall, bearing Head of beautiful woman on stick. He holds it up straight before him & marches around Man with it, continually passing under his outstretched arms. Man turns & turns in direction of Little Boy.

Little Boy runs behind Man and lisps in his ear. Man says, "What?" He turns around but Boy keeps behind him and lisps again. Man says "What?" Boy lisps again. Man says "Oh, I see, I see." Boy resumes circling Man, carrying Head of woman. Man says brightly, "Well, now, let's see. I suppose I must have been about 12. I was playing cello in the junior symphony and there was this girl on the viola that I had rather large eyes for. She used to hit those low notes and drive me out of my mind—"

Boy continues to circle Man, moving faster than before, and Man continues to turn in direction of Boy. Man says not so brightly, "Well, maybe it was earlier than that." Boy begins to cry as he circles Man. Man says, "Let's see. When I was about 10 we lived out in the Mission district. At 89 Coleridge Street. Her name was Marie Keeley. She had large eyes and sat next to me at Fairmont Grammar School on Cheney Street. I never kissed her but I gave her some gum. She used to chew the gum and stick it under the desk. Then I used to get it and chew it. I imagined we were kissing that way."

Boy with Head continues to cry as he circles further & further from Man. Man keeps turning toward Boy as he speaks slowly: "Then there was that summer we lived on a farm. I must have been 14 by then. There was this girl who used to come by with the cows every day. She had large breasts and lived up the road. I used to follow her when she came by in the evening with the cows, but she never looked at me. One time when she came by it was dusk and I heard her singing in the dusk as she went by. I don't remember her face anymore, but later, when we left the country, I used to imagine her in bed. I never knew what her name was but I used to imagine it was Marie and I used to get hot thinking about her and about a lot of other girls I knew by then, and I used to think about them as if they were all one body in bed with me or somewhere in some nameless place alone with me, but then—"

The Boy has begun running as he circles the Man. During the Man's last speech, the Boy stops at a table upon which is an old wind-up phonograph. He takes the Head off its stick & places it upright on the turntable, inserts a large crank, winds the phono & sets it revolving. As the Head revolves on the turntable, a woman's lyric voice, a torn & fragile voice, singing in catches, issues from the phono.

The Man circles closer & closer to the turning Head as the singing grows louder. The Man finds the Boy first and begins to beat him. The Boy takes the crank and defends himself with it, then drops it, and runs off.

Man stumbles & fumbles around phono as the singing grows unbearably intense. He finds the turning Head & fondles it & tries to kiss it as it turns & turns away from him. The phono begins to run down. Man searches for crank on the ground, finds it & tries to insert it in phono. He can't. The phono goes slower & slower & the singing becomes a croak. It stops with a final long groan. The Man cries: "Marie! Marie!"

(Blackout)

Swinger

A great pendulum is swinging in the darkness. It swings all the way across the hall, suspended from the center of the high ceiling. From the rear of the hall a dim spotlight now picks out the pendulum, catching it only now and then in its beam. One can now see the pendulum is a bull fiddle painted black. It is suspended by an invisible nylon cord.

The spotlight, still very dim, still playing with the pendulum, moves slowly forward in the hall until it is almost in the path of the pendulum. The light grows slightly brighter, and one can now see it is being held by a woman with long hair.

She continues to play the light upon the pendulum, catching it only now and then in her light. She moves in and out of the path of the pendulum as its arc gets shorter. Never touching it, she nevertheless manages to bring her body closer and closer to the pendulum in a kind of dance that becomes more and more sensuous. Her light has grown stronger, and one can now see she is naked. (Perhaps she was not naked when she entered but has disrobed in the dance.)

16

The pendulum has almost come to a complete rest, dead center, as she dances most sensuously up close to it, still without touching it. A climax of taped sound is reached just as the pendulum completely stops swinging and a red spot from the rear is focused on it and on her.

Suddenly with a cry she embraces the bull and pulls it to the ground. She lies down under it, embracing it passionately, with strange cries.

Sleeper

A big STRING BASS painted white, lying in a deserted place. Full moon.

Enter FIRST LOVER, right, wearing white tie and tails. Starts fooling around with BASS, fondling head and neck, stroking strings, etc. Draws bow from under tailcoat and proceeds to play very softly: Bach or Telemann.

Enter SECOND LOVER, left, wearing peg pants, tight jacket, string tie, and dark contour glasses. Circles FIRST LOVER with a sidewise, scuttling motion, finally takes bow from him, chases him off, returns slowly, circling BASS, drops bow on ground, tentatively fingers BASS, fondling neck and body, and proceeds to play Miles Davis or Ornette Coleman.

Enter FIRST LOVER, right. Picks up bow, circles SECOND LOVER, wrests BASS from him, fondles it, and proceeds to play same Bach or Telemann, louder than before, as SECOND LOVER circles him with sidewise, scuttling motion, then, very cool, lies down, takes out Zig-Zag cigarette paper and Band Aid can, fills Zig-Zag paper from can, rolls it, lights it, draws in, holds it, raises head and watches FIRST LOVER for a moment, lies back, eyes closed, smoking, rises in slow motion and circles FIRST LOVER, coolly takes

BASS from him, fondles BASS, and proceeds to play same Miles Davis or Ornette Coleman, very lyrically.

FIRST LOVER paces forth and back, twirling bow, lights a filter-tip in a cigarette holder, smokes without inhaling while circling SECOND LOVER, finally puts out cigarette, walks up to SECOND LOVER, wrests BASS from him, and proceeds to play Bach or Telemann, very eloquently.

SECOND LOVER, very cool, lies down flat, takes out Band Aid can and Zig-Zag paper, rolls another joint, lights it, draws in, holds it, lies back, eyes closed, raises head and watches FIRST LOVER, gets up slow motion and circles FIRST LOVER very slowly, then very coolly takes BASS from him, fondles BASS very tenderly, and proceeds to play John Lewis' "Django," with great feeling.

FIRST LOVER circles him, twirling bow, starts to take off tailcoat, puts it back on, takes it off, puts it back on, marches up to SECOND LOVER and roughly wrests BASS away from him, and proceeds to play Bach or Telemann again, with very great feeling.

SECOND LOVER lies down, rolls another joint, smokes, eyes closed, snapping fingers very slowly (as FIRST LOVER seems to be reaching some sort of climax), rises slowly, circles FIRST LOVER in slow motion, shedding his clothes as he goes until he is down to his tights and dark glasses, then very coolly takes BASS from FIRST LOVER, lays BASS flat on floor and lies down alongside, caressing BASS very tenderly as he plays more and more passionately, as FIRST LOVER runs to conductor's podium downstage, waves bow and raps it on podium, as SECOND LOVER embraces BASS more and more passionately, his jazz beginning to reach a climax, as FIRST LOVER raps on podium more and more violently, breaks bow, and rushes off, right, as SECOND LOVER rolls on top of BASS, crooning to BASS and embracing BASS very passionately. In sudden darkness his jass* reaches some climax; then his sound begins to falter; then silence.

In the darkness now is heard Gunther Schuller's Variant of John Lewis' "Django" (or other confrontation of jazz and classical) as FIRST LOVER, very very old now, enters in single beam of light, finds SECOND LOVER (who is now also very old) and pulls him to his feet, as recording of jazz and classical reaches point of final integration. And the two stagger off together, holding each other up.

Silence and darkness.

A single beam of light now picks out BASS, lying motionless and alone, face up.

A lion enters, comes up close and looks down at the Sleeping Gypsy. There is an effect of moonlight, very poetic.

---

*Jass: jas: jazz: jasm: gism (see Peter Tamony, "Jazz, the Word" in *Jazz: a quarterly of american music* #1, October, 1958).

The Jig Is Up

The scene: a public park in Charlotte, North Carolina. A crowd of very well-dressed Whites is strolling about under the trees, very sedately, very calmly, arm in arm.

Suddenly they fall screaming to the ground and start to crawl around and roll in great heaps of autumn leaves, roaring like animals.

Now a big empty garbage truck appears and a strange exultant wailing rises from the people as they throw themselves in front of the truck. The Negro driver blows his horn but the wailing grows louder & wilder.

The Negro scavengers descend from the truck and proceed gently to throw all the people into big burlap bags, two in each bag. Some couples, wrongly paired, scream, break and run to other partners. Finally all the Whites are loaded into bags on the truck.

The scavengers climb to their places up front, light cigars, stretch, and relax. One stretches out on the hood, smoking, eyes closed.

In the back there is a great thrashing about in the burlap bags, and the strange exultant wailing continues. It reaches a climax and suddenly dies out. In the silence the thrashing ceases. The Negro on the hood takes out a harmonica and, eyes closed, begins softly to play "Swing Low, Sweet Chariot." After a long time he stops playing. The scavengers all continue smoking silently, eyes closed, motionless.

After a long time, the driver starts his motor up very quietly. He lets it idle very quietly. Then he guns it, and the truck roars off.

The Center for Death

Scene: a tropical island. A billboard sign reads:

COME HERE TO DIE
CENTER FOR DEATH
TERMINAL CASES ONLY
Not For Everyone

Another sign reads:

READY TO DIE?

WHAT IS YOUR ECSTASY COUNT

ON THE EXISTENTIAL TYPEWRITER?

    Enter a Doctor with stethoscope, wheeling a medicine chest. He stops & inspects various bottles in the chest.
    Enter a traveling Watch Salesman with open suitcase in which watches are displayed. He holds up watches & shouts "Time! Time!"
    Enter a Veiled Woman dressed in nothing but brassieres. Her body is completely covered with brassieres, and she wears a dozen brassieres over her breasts, one on top of the other. She proceeds to take them off as she walks about.

23

Each time she takes one off, she holds it high above her head and cries or sings "Life! Life!"

Enter a Masked Man dressed in nothing but jockstraps. His body is completely covered with jockstraps, and he wears a dozen jockstraps over his crotch, one on top of the other. He proceeds to take them off as he marches about, crying "Life! Life!"

These persons fall into a single line behind the Doctor & pace slowly in a circle behind him. He passes pills from different bottles to each of them. These they slowly swallow. From time to time the Watch Salesman steps down into the audience & hauls someone into the procession, or tries to, crying "Time! Time!"

Enter a Sax Player blowing a funeral dirge. He joins the line, swallows pills, and after a while begins blowing a very strange & lyrical refrain.

Enter a Blind Apple Seller with a big basket of apples, crying "I sell girls' breasts! I sell girls' breasts!" He joins the line, still hawking, and takes pills.

They all continue to follow the Doctor around in single file, slowly pacing in a big circle, each continuing his own private routine, each wailing his or her own message. Their voices rise in a broken kind of litany. When the Veiled Woman is down to her last brassiere, she throws off her veil & stands revealed as a skinny old hag. When the Masked Man is down to his last jockstrap, he throws off his clown's mask & stands revealed as a skinny old man. Their wailing grows louder, the sax wails louder. The scene grows darker but a curious light illuminates their transfigured faces. Eyes closed as they walk more & more slowly, they speak words:

Watch Salesman: "Tick of consciousness! Stoned strokes—"
Unveiled Woman: "Sweet silent thought—"
Sax Player: "Baboon dreams! Robot perceptions!"
Unmasked Man: "Ecstasies of absurdity—"
Apple Seller: "Paper bones, paper flesh, someone inside—"
Unveiled Woman: "Light in me! Clear light! Body of Radiance!"
Unmasked man: "Things into Emptiness—"
Apple Seller: "Someone inside! Flame life!"
The Doctor distributes lighted candles to all as they walk. He leads the first of them off into the surrounding darkness. One by one they pass into it, holding the candles before them, eyes closed. The sax wails in unknown ecstasy. The Watch Salesman is the last to go. He sticks his lighted candle in his fly and holds up an enormous clock to the audience, screaming "Time! Time!" Silence falls on the scene, the Watch Salesman motionless with clock still upraised. His candle drips white wax. A curlew cries in the end of day. Gone into that place of enormous ignorance . . . .

(Blackout)

Non-Objection

A large studio with four very large white canvases set up in a square, facing forward, ten feet apart. The back wall of the studio is solid black. On each side of studio, a very large white baby carriage. In front, center, a bathtub on the floor, full of black paint. Sprawled in the tub, with arms and legs hanging over, a dead nude model.

FIRST REAL PAINTER rises with a single ecstatic cry from baby carriage, right, pulls large handmirror from back pocket and looks at self, pulls large paintbrush from other back pocket, dips it in tub and proceeds to paint small crude faces in black on first canvas at right, looking in mirror between strokes, as

SECOND REAL PAINTER rises with a single ecstatic cry from baby carriage, left, pulls large handmirror from back pocket and looks at self, pulls large paintbrush from other back pocket, dips it in tub and proceeds to paint small simple faces on first canvas at left, looking in mirror between strokes, as

FIRST REAL PAINTER stops and looks at what other painter is painting and then starts painting bigger and bigger black faces on his canvas, as

SECOND REAL PAINTER stops and looks at what other painter is painting and then starts painting bigger and bigger black faces on his canvas, as

FIRST REAL PAINTER gets his canvas completely covered with faces, all the while looking at his handmirror between strokes, and finally with a great stroke knocks canvas over and jumps over it to second canvas on his side, as

SECOND REAL PAINTER does same on his side, as

FIRST REAL PAINTER looks in handmirror and proceeds to cover his second canvas with black squares, as

SECOND REAL PAINTER does same on his second canvas, as

FIRST REAL PAINTER sees what other painter is painting and looks in handmirror and proceeds to paint much larger and blacker squares on his canvas, as

SECOND REAL PAINTER does same, as

FIRST REAL PAINTER picks up broom, dips it in tub and proceeds to sweep his canvas with black paint, until canvas is almost solid black, as

SECOND REAL PAINTER does same, as

FIRST REAL PAINTER knocks over his second canvas with a single great stroke and jumps over it to find himself confronted with solid black wall which he attacks with the broom, flailing wildly at it, as

SECOND REAL PAINTER does same on his side, as

FIRST REAL PAINTER begins roaring as he flails the wall more and more violently, as

SECOND REAL PAINTER does same.

Both REAL PAINTERS fall exhausted and lie motionless.

Two hooded figures in black rush in, trundling a coffin on wheels, pile both REAL PAINTERS into coffin, slam lid, and wheel them off, crying, "The End! The End!"

FLOORPLAN FOR "NON-OBJECTION"

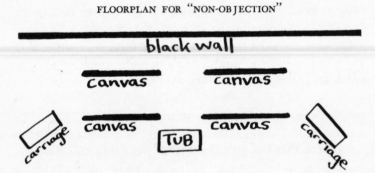

Ha-Ha

Cinematic Prologue

The main avenue of a European city. Close-up of street sign UNTER DEN LINDEN. Frost and icicles indicate zero weather. Cut off at the waist by the top of the screen, nurse girls push baby carriages in procession. The hoods of the carriages have numbers pinned upon them, like bicycle riders. The motion accelerates.

As each carriage arrives in front of a rathskeller door, a large boot, attached to a leg which is partly off-screen, kicks it into the air. The babies, with faces muffled, describe long parabolas, pass through cirrus clouds, and land in the north Atlantic. One by one they are run down by the camouflaged cruisers.

(From a scenario by Elliot Paul, published in *transition*, February, 1928)

A Statue of Liberty, center. It faces left, with torch up-raised and burning. In rear-end of Statue, a large square hole with an iron door hinged to it. A hot fire burns within and smoke pours from a stack that sticks out of Statue's back. To the right, a few paces behind Statue, a huge pile of baby dolls of all colors, with a flag on a pole stuck into it.

In the distance, off right, muffled explosions, now and then interspersed with antique martial music. From time to time, a large free monkey or gibbon enters from behind Statue, looks around, says "Ha-Ha," and exits behind Statue.

A Rowboat appears, left, loaded with women. They look Trojan. Each has a large, naked doll strapped to her bosom in a transparent net. (A few carry their babies low on their bodies so that, seen through the transparent nets, they appear still to be in the uterus.) One by one they disembark, circle Statue, approach pile of babies, kneel and place their own babies on pile, turn and dance off, right. Large monkey or gibbon on chain appears from behind Statue, looks around, says "Ha-Ha," picks up coal shovel and furiously shovels babies into stoke hole in Statue. Chain pulls monkey off behind Statue. Torch burns brighter. A Laughing Record is heard distantly, as

Second Rowboat appears, left, loaded with women with babies in transparent nets. They look European. Each descends, circles Statue, approaches pile of babies, kneels and places baby on pile, turns and staggers off, right. Large monkey on chain appears from behind Statue, looks around, says "Ha-Ha," picks up shovel and stokes fire with babies. Chain pulls him off, as Laughing Record is heard louder than before, and torch begins to dim. Heavier smoke pours from stack, and torch sputters as

Workmen in tin hats run in, right, carrying ladders and coils of wire which they proceed to string from torch to offstage right. They fix large bulb in top of torch and run off, right. The bulb comes on, very bright, Laughing Record is heard, monkey enters, same routine, and monkey is pulled off as City Bus appears, right, loaded with women with babies. They look like the Twenties. Fox-trots can be heard as they leave babies on pile and run off, right, as bulb grows dimmer, Laughing Record is heard, and monkey enters. Same routine, and monkey is pulled off as

Workmen re-enter, right, staggering under huge coils of wire, with huge bulbs of all colors and neon tubes. They enmesh Statue in coils and affix huge bulbs everywhere on it, including neon signs and flashing traffic signals. Muffled explosions are heard, off right, as the men rush through their work and rush off, right. Martial music is heard, interspersed with distant cheering, as bulbs and signs all burn bright, then begin to dim, then begin to flicker, then begin to blink on and off. The explosions grow louder and closer. More bulbs go out with each explosion. Gradually the explosions cease as the last lights go out. The Laughing Record is heard, distantly, but is cut off suddenly.

Silence and darkness. Somewhere, very distantly, a band plays a cool jazz version of the National Anthem of whatever country we are in.

An Evening at the Carnival

A carnival booth.

American Diplomat (in dress coat cut from American flag) inside of booth, chewing bubble gum, blowing bubbles and blowing up balloons. Inflated balloons pile up until whole booth is filled with them.

Diplomat keeps blowing up balloons and blowing bubbles and laughing uproariously. Each time he blows, the sound of a bugle is heard throughout the land.

American Soldier's Head in helmet appears among balloons. Diplomat ties an inflated balloon to Soldier's helmet, puts an uninflated balloon in Soldier's mouth and shouts incomprehensible, improvised slogans. Soldier blows furiously into balloon and sinks from sight among other balloons as he inflates his.

Same routine with each of following heads:
American Indian in headdress
Mexican in sombrero
Negro Statesman in top hat
Arab in fez

Oriental Soldier
German Soldier
Each sinks from sight in turn.

A *barbudo* (*Fidelista*) appears. Same routine, only *Fidelista* blows up and pops balloon which Diplomat puts in his mouth. Diplomat falls over on his face when balloon pops. *Fidelista* then pulls out his own huge balloon (which is painted half red & half white) & blows & blows, as *mariachi* music is heard, alternated with sound of a small brass band playing the *Internationale*. Each time the *Internationale* sounds, *Fidelista* sinks lower & lower, still blowing. Each time the *mariachi* music reasserts itself, *Fidelista* rises up again, still blowing. Voices can be heard singing the *Internationale* as *Fidelista* almost sinks from sight. Then the *mariachi* music sounds again & drowns out the *Internationale*. Then the *Internationale* drowns out the *mariachis*. This goes on indefinitely. Perhaps the native music will sound again & *Fidelista* rise again. No one knows how it will end.

Bearded Lady "Dies"

Sprouts Wings
and Flies Off

UNKNOWN PILOT STEALS SHOW

A strange and beautiful but very hairy young woman fainted in front of a fashionable downtown gallery yesterday where an "opening" was in progress.

The unidentified lady was carried into the gallery and stripped of her clothes by the German artist whose paintings were being presented but who nevertheless refused to divulge his name. (The paintings were announced to have been painted "anonymously," but critics immediately dubbed him Anonymous Bosch.)

The lady then was placed on a seesaw, and unsuccessful attempts were made to arouse her by rocking the seesaw. "Anonymous" then proceeded to paint her as she lay almost upright on the seesaw. He painted a huge face on the lady's front side, making the breasts into eyes, and the completed painting was seen to resemble the notorious Bearded Lady of old-time circuses.

When the artist was completely finished, he suddenly disappeared behind scenes, and the "Bearded Lady" who had still not revived was carried out again into the street and laid on the sidewalk. A sheet was placed over her, and a funeral march began playing on a loudspeaker.

A considerable crowd had by this time gathered, and the police were called, but at this moment a helicopter (some reports said it was a hearse) appeared out of Nowhere with a tall, bearded man in helmet and goggles at the controls. The unidentified pilot descended, carrying a large wood cross and a knapsack, approached the reclining lady, took a pair of rubber waterwings from his sack, fastened them to the lady, and proceeded to blow up the wings by blowing into the lady's mouth, much in the manner of mouth-to-mouth resuscitation. This took a long time, and there was some question as to what he (or they) were actually doing since the lady seemed to be stimulated in certain ways, even though not actually revived. (Some observers even maintained they perceived a distinct swelling of the lady's lower abdomen, as if she were growing pregnant before their eyes.) However, when the wings were finally fully inflated, the pilot proceeded to stretch the lady on the wood cross, dragged it and her to the helicopter (or hearse), lifted her off the cross, and stowed her inside.

He then climbed aboard and drove or flew off down the street, waving at the stunned crowd and making the Sign of the Cross. (The cross itself was later impounded and found to be of a hard, unidentifiable wood that grows only in the mountains.)

The combined forces of police, FBI, and CIA are probing the symbolic meaning of this strange incident which is thought to be part of a sinister international plot of some kind.

Servants of the People

"Swept with con the millions stood under the signs"
—William Burroughs

A stage is not needed. Any place people assemble will do. But the more distinguished the location the better. A large, respectable audience is to be preferred to one made up of poets, artists and their ilk.

In each corner of the meeting place is an elevated podium, with a loudspeaker mounted on it as if it were the head of an orator. A spotlight is also mounted on each podium, but at the moment all is in darkness.

Sound of a large public meeting going on: babel of voices, cheers, clapping, gavel-pounding, etc. Individual voices begin to distinguish themselves, although it is impossible to tell the real actors from the rest of the audience. Some are just naturally good actors, some just naturally bad actors.

VARIOUS VOICES (*in audience*): . . . Mr. Chairman . . . duly constituted . . . rights of the . . . people . . . and their duly constituted . . . liberty . . . Mr. Chairman . . . if you will allow me . . . Mr. Chairman, if I may have the floor at this time . . . for one minute . . . as a duly

36

constituted . . . as guaranteed in . . . member of the
. . . Bill of Rights . . . according to the standing rules
of this . . . rules of parliamentary procedure . . . Mr.
Chairman, I propose . . . If I may propose . . . I re-
peat . . . Let us . . . here and now . . . once and for all
. . . The Congress of the United States is . . . is not
. . . The Senate . . . If I may be allowed one further
observation . . . in the name of . . . Mr. Chairman . . .
I demand . . . I . . . We . . . who . . . We who . . .

VOICES ON FIRST LOUDSPEAKER (*garbled, in darkness*): With
. . . malice . . . towards . . . with charity for . . . Let us
strive on to a just . . . and lasting peace . . . In the
future days which we seek to make secure . . . we look
. . . we look forward to a . . . world founded upon four
essential free . . . freedoms . . . For Congress shall . . .
make no law . . . For we hold these truths to be . . .
self-ev . . . For . . . liberty and jus . . . justice for . . .
In the name of the . . . (*Various Voices continue in
darkness as before.*)

VOICE ON SECOND LOUDSPEAKER: (*A dim white light illuminates the podium from below and remains on.*) And,
Mr. Speaker, by unwavering faith in the inherent
greatness of the American character and in the pas-
sion for justice possessed by most Americans who have
come forth from time to time, giving direction and
leadership to the people of this country in time of
tribulation and peril. . . .

VOICE ON THIRD LOUDSPEAKER: (*A dim light illuminates the
podium from below and remains on.*) The question
then recurs: What is the cause of this discontent? It
will be found in the belief of the people of the Southern States, as prevalent as discontent itself, that they

cannot remain, as things now are, consistently with honor and safety, in the Union. The next question to be considered is: What has caused this belief? What . . .

(*A small white spotlight from an elevated position picks out a Young Man and Woman embracing passionately in the middle of a front row.*)

VOICE ON FOURTH LOUDSPEAKER: (*A dim light illuminates the podium and remains on.*) And I am indeed honored to recall to you that our speaker for tonight has been the recipient of the Certificate of Merit for great and inspiring public service in the Patriotic Sons of America, as well as the Special Citation for outstanding public service of the American Coalition of Patriotic Societies, as well as the Medal of Honor of the Order of the Founders and Patriots of America, as well as the much-coveted Citation of Merit and Distinction of the National Women's Patriotic Conference on National Defense, and also the Certificate of Merit of the Daughters of the . . .

(*Young Man and Woman continue to embrace, very passionately, the spotlight still on them.*)

GRADUATE STUDENT (*in front row*): Mr. Chairman . . . Mr. Speaker . . . Mr. Chairman . . . Sir . . . May I . . . May I have the floor? I would like to . . . I have a few . . .

(*Light fades from Young Man and Woman.*)

VOICE ON FIRST LOUDSPEAKER: (*A dim light illuminates the podium and remains on.*) Ah, but, let us not despair. America will win through in the end. All goes well, even if at moments we are attacked by petty dissenters who can find nothing but scorn to heap upon our democracy. Despite what they say, we are still the freest country in the world. And I am not asking you to try Russia for a comparison. Try France, try England, try where you will. In spite of what they say, ours is a great nation forging ahead to goals and achievements for the common man, and by the common man, which we ourselves have hardly dreamed of. In spite of all, we are . . .

(*Small white spot picks out Young Man and Woman who are now, hand in hand, making their way across a row.*)

YOUNG MAN AND WOMAN: Excuse us, please . . . Excuse me . . . Sorry . . . We're . . .

GRADUATE STUDENT: (*Spot shifts to him as he mounts chair and faces audience.*) Mr. Chairman, Mr. Chairman! After all, there is some other point of view. I don't want to be called a petty dissenter, but there are, after all, other valid points of view. And there really is very little reason for optimism at this time. . . . (*Light fades from him.*)

VOICE ON SECOND LOUDSPEAKER: Yes, money talks, ladies and gentlemen, money talks, and if there is to be money, it's going to talk, and there will be, let me assure you, ladies and gentlemen, *chaos in concrete.* . . .

(*White spot picks out Young Man and Woman now making their way across another row.*)

YOUNG MAN AND WOMAN: Excuse us . . . Pardon . . . Pardon
me . . . We're just . . . So sorry . . . We'd like to . . .
(*Light fades from them.*)

VOICE ON THIRD LOUDSPEAKER: Mr. President, Anne Jarvis,
of Groton, West Virginia, was the founder of
Mother's Day, but to all mankind every day is
Mother's Day, and tender and beautiful words have
been written and spoken about the hand that rocks
the cradle rules the world, and we . . .

GRADUATE STUDENT: (*White spot picks him out.*) I repeat,
there is very little reason for optimism in this crisis,
very little. I don't care what the ratio of telegrams is.
The facts of the last week show that the nation-
states, the national leaders, the people of the United
States, are fantastically involved in the assumptions,
goals, tactics, morality of the Cold War, and that this
fantastic involvement has only one course and one
end. . . .

SECOND STUDENT (*trying to pull Graduate Student down
from his chair*): Oh, for Christ's sake . . . Let's get
the hell out of here. What the fuck you want to hang
around here for? (*Light fades from them.*)

VOICE ON FOURTH LOUDSPEAKER: Just where exactly we stand
in space is something . . . (*Spotlight picks out Young
Man and Woman making their way across another
row, and follows them as speaker continues*) . . .
something which should concern not only those of us
in aviation but also every single one of you here,

whose very lives are in the balance, and therefore I do yield five minutes to my distinguished colleague from Idaho. As to the resolution of the Kansas Livestock Commission, I want to propose the following. I want to announce to my constituents everywhere that this is Soil Conservation Week in Colorado, and that means just two things, two big things, and I think you will all agree that . . . what this country needs . . . is a . . .

GRADUATE STUDENT: (*Spot picks him out still standing on chair facing audience.*) For there could be but one course and one end for such fantastic insanity, and yet it is insanity itself which is considered most sane these days. . . .

SECOND STUDENT (*trying to pull him down as before*): Come on! What're we wasting our time around here for? Let's get going.

(*Spot fades from them and picks up* Young Man *and* Woman *now making their way across another row.*)

YOUNG MAN AND WOMAN: Sorry! We're just trying to get . . . Excuse me, we're just . . . trying to . . . get out . . . we just want to . . . please . . . (*Light fades from them.*)

VOICE ON FIRST LOUDSPEAKER: (*Small red spotlight on podium plays on audience during this speech.*) Now, the hearings which begin today are in furtherance of the powers and duties of the Committee pursuant to Public Law 601 of the 79th Congress which not only establishes the basic jurisdiction of the Committee

but also mandates the Committee to exercise continu-
ous watchfulness of the execution of any laws the
subject of which is within the jurisdiction of this
Committee. . . .

GRADUATE STUDENT: (*White spot picks him out again.*)
And the tragedy is that we *have* to be concerned with
these people, these men with dirty hands. In this
morning's edition of The New York Times you see a
picture of our smiling delegates at the U.N., and the
most annoying thing about this whole thing is that
you have to leave your family, or your life, you have
to stop worrying about making love or writing poems
or reading books, and you have to watch a television
set during such crises to see *these* people defend *your*
freedom, your peace, your way of life. What do they
know about that way of life? What . . .

SECOND STUDENT (*still trying to pull him down*): Ah, hell!
(*Mounts his own chair and faces audience.*) Yeah,
well, all you old farts out there take notice—I for one
have had enough, see? I'm fed up, understand? I have
seen the best minds of my generation swept with
con. . . . (*Light fades from them.*)

VOICE ON SECOND LOUDSPEAKER: (*During this speech, a
white spot illuminates Young Man and Woman again
making their way across another row.*) Time out now
for a special announcement from J. Edgar Hoover,
Director of the Federal Bureau of Investigation,
brought to you as a public service: *Boys and girls!*
For your protection, memorize the following rules.
One: Turn down gifts from strangers. Two: Refuse
rides offered by strangers. Three: Avoid dark and
lonely streets. Four: Know your local policeman. . . .

YOUNG MAN AND WOMAN: Excuse us, please . . . We're just trying to make our way . . . out . . . please . . . sorry . . . We're just . . . We just want to . . . please . . . if we could only . . . (*Light fades from them.*)

VOICE ON FIRST LOUDSPEAKER: (*During this speech, the small red spotlight on podium comes on again and picks out members of the audience.*) And in response to this power and duty, this Committee is continuously in the process of accumulating factual information respecting Communists, the Communist Party and Communist activities which will enable the Committee and the Congress to appraise the administration and operation of the Smith Act, the Internal Security Act and the . . .

(*Various Voices in audience shout* "Hear, hear!" *Others cheer.*)

GRADUATE STUDENT: (*Spotlight, now changed to red, picks him out.*) And one has to conclude that there was no military basis whatever for the President's action. Then what was the basis? The basis was the wholesale acceptance of the myths of the Cold War. The wholesale acceptance that nothing the United States does can be wrong. Now, that seems like an incredible thing to say about any nation in any historical period. Yet we find our liberal spokesmen maintaining precisely that. . . .

(*Various Voices in audience shout* "Aw, shut up!" *Others boo.*)

SECOND STUDENT (*mounting his chair and facing audience again*): Yeah, and that ain't all! It's all a big con, hear me? Your whole big dreary scene is a great big hairy drag, a sad scene if I ever saw one, what I mean! And I for one am getting out, understand? I for one've had enough of your fat-ass civilization. I'm cutting out for faraway scenes, so fuck all of you and your great big evil system! Blow yourselves up, see if I give a fuck, I for one won't be around for the funeral, you and your . . . big . . . (*He ducks out as light fades.*)

VOICE ON THIRD LOUDSPEAKER (*very calmly*): Mr. Speaker, there are always those poor prophets of doom who announce that an epidemic of world lawlessness is spreading and that no one will escape. "Let no one imagine," they cry, "that America will escape or that it may expect mercy or that this Western Hemisphere will not be attacked and that it will continue tranquilly and peacefully to carry on the ethics and arts of civilization." Ah, but Mr. Speaker, may I urge our great people to reject these prophets of gloom and doom. For I would remind you all that America has weathered worse storms and worse crises than this, and America will weather this one. America was not built in a day, and the stepping stones of greatness have been surely set in place, and the foundation stones are not about to crumble, for the foundation stones of our still-free and still-profoundly democratic society, the foundation stones are the people themselves, and the people themselves still rise up whenever the occasion demands it, the people themselves can still stand up to any threat from within or without, the people themselves are still in control. . . .

VOICE ON FOURTH LOUDSPEAKER: (*A larger red spotlight mounted on podium focuses on various faces in audience during this speech.*) Now, Mr. Secretary, when you issued your apology, when you issued your press release repudiating the Air Force publication and issued your apology to the National Council of Churches of Christ in the U.S.A., did you mean by that act to convey the impression that the Air Force was convinced that the National Council of Churches was *not* infiltrated by fellow travelers? Or that the Communist Party had *not* . . .

(*Various Voices cry* "Hear, hear!" *Others cheer.*)

YOUNG MAN AND WOMAN: (*Spotlight, now changed to red, picks them out stumbling across another row.*) Please . . . we're just trying to . . . we'd like to get out, if . . . Pardon . . . very sorry . . . We can't seem to . . . Please let us through . . . We have to . . . We must get away . . . please . . . (*Light fades from them.*)

GRADUATE STUDENT: (*Red spotlight picks him out.*) . . . that there is nothing the United States can do on the borders of another nation that can be called war-like. Nothing. Now, this is truly incredible . . . to find articulate spokesmen of liberal dissent in this country maintaining this. There is no dialogue on these questions in the United States. Nobody of substance will get up and attack the assumptions of the Cold War. No one. No Stevenson, no Bowles, no Dean Rusk will get up and say . . . (*Light fades from him.*)

VOICE ON FIRST LOUDSPEAKER: (*Slow drawl. During this speech, a brighter red spotlight focuses on various*

faces in audience.) I am—uh—not concerned with—
We are not concerned with—uh—specific instances of
who goes to jail as a result of—uh—a hearing. That's—
uh—a coincidence, as far as we're concerned. That's
not the object of—uh—our hearings. If someone—uh—
happens to have—uh—invoked the Constitutional—
uh—privilege improperly or abused it—uh—why, that's
—uh—a matter of law for the Department of Justice—
but—if it does happen, it's not *our* making. Our records are submitted to the Department of Justice, and
we don't—uh—prosecute anybody. So we're not concerned here about that—the Commies—of course say
this is just an exposé—uh—that again is just—uh—an
incidental thing. . . .

(*Cries of* "Hear, hear!" *Clapping.*)

GRADUATE STUDENT: (*Larger red spot picks him out.*) No
one will get up and say, We are no more fighting for
freedom and democracy with our missiles than they
are. No one will say that we are supporting dictator-
ships as well as they are. No one will say that we are
playing the same dangerous game. And this is the true
tragedy. . . .

(*Various Voices shout* "Go away!" *Others boo. Light fades
from him.*)

YOUNG MAN AND WOMAN: (*Red spot picks them out making their way across another row.*) Please . . . please
. . . we're . . . please let us through . . . we want to get
out . . . we have to . . . get away . . . please . . . Let
us out! . . . (*Light fades from them.*)

VOICE ON SECOND LOUDSPEAKER: (*During this speech, a large red spotlight focuses on middle-aged woman up front and flash-bulbs go off in front of her.*) Now, I expect in the course of this investigation to cover a number of areas with you, madam. At the outset, I should like to ask you first of all, Have you ever been a member of the Communist Party, when did you join the Communist Party, and when did you finally irrevocably disassociate yourself from the Communist Party?

WOMAN: Please, I am very nervous when pictures are taken. Please, I ask that no pictures be taken. . . . You promised there would be no pictures and no TV, according to your own rules . . . please . . . (*She ducks out of spotlight which now sweeps the audience. Confused voices begin to be heard.*)

GRADUATE STUDENT: (*Red spot settles on him.*) What happened to the liberals in this country? I ask you, what has happened to them? We have been betrayed. We have been betrayed by articulate intellectuals, we have been betrayed by men who know better. There were twenty people who refused to speak here today. Where are our liberal leaders? We are in a dangerous way because we have no one to rally behind. We have no media, we have no person of prominence in our country who will lead us in any sort of campaign. There is no dialogue. We have no basis for conducting one. And this is the true sadness of our position. . . .

(*Light fades from him. A hum of confused voices becomes more audible as red spot continues to search the audience. Young Man and Woman can be seen still stumbling across a row near the rear and crying out.*)

VOICES ON ALL LOUDSPEAKERS: (*During these speeches several more red spotlights in elevated positions are turned on audience which grows more and more restless.*) Within the Communist Party . . . Within the framework of the Communist Party . . . Within the framework of the Communist operation, is there room for concepts of God and spiritual values as we are taught them at our mother's knee? . . . Are you or have you ever been a member of the Communist Party in any capacity whatever? . . . Are you a member of any organization that is dedicated to the destruction of religion . . . dedicated to the destruction, that is, of the entire Judeo-Christian concept upon which this nation is founded? Are you a member of any organization which is an atheistic organization dedicated to the destruction of all concepts of God and the sterility of the individual? Are you or are you not now a member of . . .

GRADUATE STUDENT: (*Red spot focuses on him. He shouts to be heard.*) And for us, for those of us here who respect the ideals and really thought there was a difference between the United States and the Soviet Union and/or China—and I am one—for those of us who thought that the United States was a different sort of country with an internal dialogue on foreign policy, with people of prominence who could and would speak out—it is for those of us now to say we have been betrayed, we too have been betrayed, by *our* American revolution and *our* leaders—and by you —by you, sirs—you up there on your platforms— (*He points into the red lights.*) By all of you up there— you in your high places, in the places of control, you with your gavels, you with the—

(Hum of confused voices grows still louder as red spots increase in brilliance and sweep audience. The increased red light allows us to see that the lights are now held by hooded figures. Sound of violent gavel-pounding and cries of "Order, order!")

VOICES ON ALL LOUDSPEAKERS: Are you or are you not a member of atheistic Judo-Christian police organization Communist Party Communist underground under our mother's knee upon which this great nation was founded or have you ever been hard-core Communists infiltrating friendly witness or cooperate with police answer Committee counsel or run the risk of godless conspiracy controlled by police foreign powers international Communist police conspiracy offer you one last chance to answer questions your membership in the Communist Party Communist Party Operation Abolition Are you now or have you ever been a member of . . . a great nation . . . hard-core . . . Commie . . . Communist Commie . . . Communist . . . Ca-ca . . .

(Sirens are sounded and floodlights or houselights flashed on. The figures holding the red lights have thrown off their hoods and are now seen to be wearing boots, motorcycle crash helmets, and goggles, and their now-blinding lights are seen to be fixed in the nozzles of large fire-hoses which are extended as they advance upon the audience, roaring and blowing whistles. Sirens sound over the loudspeakers as the audience is hustled and herded out. Many flee; others put up a struggle or go limp and have to be carried out.)

BORE

Routines never end; they have to be broken. This little routine to end all routines requires the formation of a worldwide society dedicated to the non-violent disruption of institutionalized events, a little international conspiracy for the non-violent "disturbance of the peace." That is, the peace of daily routines, traditional functions, business-as-usual in a fuckedup universe . . . the peace of the police and the peace of politicians (which is a piece of con), the peace of senators in their dotage who ought to be retired to Arizona at age 50, the peace of the two great political parties on the same side with no party on the other side of the peace and none allowed, the peace of Ford Foundation theatre directors and the peace of $16,000-a-year professors making their living on $1,000-a-year poets, the peace of young retired poets & old retired poets with poems about climbing down from the barricades which they never mounted in the first place, the peace of mindless painters hiding behind a scorn for words, the peace of the *Paris Review* and the *Kenyon Review* and the *Sewanee Review* and the *Hudson Review* and the peace of *Poetry* Chicago, and the peace of Westchester County and the peace of Palo Alto, and the peace of the short-haired hyenas of

American big business, and the peace of parents who have
sown their wild seeds & seen them grow up into potted
plants, the horny bachelors of indifference of Sausalito. . . .

This little subversive organization to be known as B.O.R.E.
(Brotherhood of Radical Enlightenment?)—BORE dedicated to the creation of "situations" in public places whenever some social, political or cultural event needs to be
protested against due to its fatuousness, general stupidity,
innocuousness, or whatever else offensive to the open mind
& spirit. BORE to bore from within by staging unan-
nounced spontaneous disruptions of, for instance, boring
or intellectually bankrupt plays by famous playwrights or
theatre groups, whether avant-garde or rear (with reper-
tories aimed at suburban subscription audiences). Or, for
instance, mumbled poetry readings and experimental films
held together only by the transparent celluloid of hip inco-
herence. (The first successful Bore-in was staged in San
Francisco during a screening of *Blond Cobra*, shortly after
a resolution to form a local chapter of BORE was presented
by the author at the San Francisco New School, June,
1964.)

It is to be hoped that Bore-ins will spread like legalized
marihuana on the lawn of the White House, with BORE
members necessarily unknown until they actually disrupt
some event that needs Boring Into . . . a "semi-secret"
society in other words of those who for one reason or
another want to see certain traditions or institutions in
their own particular fields shook-up. . . . Bore-in participants,
for instance, to arrive with bugles, drums & flutes under

their coats, and then to bring them forth at climactic moments in the proceedings and proceed to cry havoc . . . And bad productions & bad scenes in general everywhere in the world at all levels of activity to be warned in advance of possible Bore-ins unless things improve . . . Other variations of Bore-ins to be improvised to fit particular impasses of being & existence, for instance as follows:

The scene: a large church or cathedral of one of the established medieval faiths. Enter Chief Bore (a thin man in loincloth) carrying a water pistol. He fills it at Holy Water fount & proceeds to baptize statues & worshipers with Holy Water from his holy gun. Bores in the pews chant & sing: "We want God! We want God! We want God!" (Anything may be substituted for the word "God," depending on what one has in mind for eternity: love, life, Enovid or enlightenment.) Chief Bore mounts to pulpit and begins sermon: "Brethren, we take our text today from the Old Testament itself. Repeat after me. If God is not dead, let Him now come down at last. We have waited and waited long enough. Let there be light at last! Why this eternal gloom? Unstain the glass! Lift off the gargoyle roof and let Him come down!" (etc., etc.) . . . Priests & police come running. Chief Bore holds them off with Holy Water but in the end they crucify him.